37 Days

to

Launch

Dedicated to my parents, Wendy and Alan Duques.
While they didn't teach me much about starting a business, they
taught me everything else.

37 Days to Launch

Copyright © 2011, 2023 by Ryan Duques

All Rights Reserved

For information about permissions to reproduce selections from this book, write to ryan.duques@gmail.com

By Ryan Duques
Marisa Nadolny, editor
Cover design by Dreamscapes Design Group, Essex, Connecticut

Published by Ryan Duques
PO Box 1125
Madison, Connecticut 06443

Introduction

I am not operating under optimal conditions.

I'm telling you this first to make the point that even if you are stressed, tired, or have too many things on your plate, you, too, can start a new business, start to finish, in 37 days.

I am 35 years old but feel older. I have two beautiful blue-eyed little girls who currently allow me about five hours of sleep per night. As a serial entrepreneur, I oversee three startup companies with various business partners. To say that my life is a juggling act probably doesn't quite cover it.

But still, I absolutely love every day. It isn't "work" to me. It's who I am.

Growing up I thought I wanted to be a pilot (and a fireman, a federal agent, and a Coast Guardsman). For years I dreamed of taking to the skies every day. Had I followed my childhood dream and become a pilot I would have been miserable. Sitting in a seat for hours and hours with nothing to do but check my heading and adjust the cabin pressure every day? That would have driven me nuts. I need to keep moving (preferably on terra firma), and I get distracted easily (not a good trait in a pilot). I suspect I might even have adult ADD (I hope I finish this book).

I fit the definition of an entrepreneur long before I knew what that word meant or that it was a real job. Now, I've come to realize just how afflicted I am with this "disease," this yearning, this compulsion to constantly dream up new ventures. Just thinking about it gets me excited.

Do you have an idea for a venture? Something you've been

kicking around for a few years? Or maybe it's something you just thought of? No biggie, because if you are passionate about an idea, only one thing will ensure it never happens: non-execution. No matter how strong or weak an idea; no matter how well an idea is capitalized; whether the smartest people are involved or not, nothing matters unless there is someone there to get things started—to make decisions, and make them quickly. That person is probably you.

This short book is about identifying an opportunity, making decisions quickly and starting a business in 37 days. As you will see, most of the decisions we had to make were not anticipated— many of them were wrong and needed to be reevaluated. But all of them were made within 37 days, and they ultimately resulted in a successful launch.

I've regretted not chronicling past start-up ventures. There is no doubt that I have forgotten (and possibly purposely blocked) a great majority of the events and emotions that were part of starting some of my businesses. These notes are invaluable as a serial entrepreneur. (They also can be entertaining.) My objective here is to share with you, and the future me, the events that took place and tools I used to get SavingsClique.com launched.

An Entrepreneur at Birth

By any measure, I am afflicted with serial entrepreneurism. I am addicted to it. Like that impulse to have one more doughnut, my drive to conceive business ideas is visceral. I love every piece of conceiving, dreaming, constructing, and executing the creation of a new enterprise. For as long as I can remember, I have been compelled to start cash-generating enterprises. My parents often remind me that as a seven-year-old I would set up shop in their kitchen and sell them coffee in the morning. Of course, they already owned the coffee, but they knew better than to try to negotiate with an eager seven-year-old before their first cup of the day.

Since then I have started, in one form or another, more than a dozen businesses. Few were wildly successful, but I have no regrets about any of them. Each experience added to my knowledge base and reinforced my resolve to listen to my intuition and follow my gut.

My most powerful and successful entrepreneurial experience (to date, of course) was starting Shore Publishing, a company that grew from one quarterly community newspaper to 16 weekly newspapers in Connecticut. I formed this company with my business partner, James Warner, in his parents' dining room when we were 18 years old and still in high school. Before age 25, the company was generating revenue in excess of $1 million. Before I turned 30, our revenues were approaching $6 million and we had decided to sell the chain of papers to another independent newspaper publisher.

Even though we executed strategic decisions at Shore Publishing with resolve and relative speed, the story of that venture took place over years, not days. Nothing wrong with that, but I won't live forever, so I cannot allow each success to take 13 years. My goal is to use my experience, intuition, gut, experience, and passion to streamline my entrepreneurial experiences.

Here is my current strategy:

- Brainstorm often
- Execute quickly
- Kill bad ideas fast
- Push good ideas forward through smart leverage

I want my entrepreneurial experiences to be measured in days and weeks. Whether it's a success or a massive fail, I want to know quickly. While not every brainstorm will result in a venture that can be developed and launched in less than two months, *some do*, and this is the story of one of them.

They Said it would Never Last: My Unlikely Partnership With James

To understand how this business was crafted in just 37 days, I need to introduce you to my business partner, James Warner. James has been my business partner since we were 10 years old. It sounds silly, but it's true. An entire (long) book could be written on this unlikely partnership formed between neighborhood friends.

Starting with lawn care and VHS transfer services we were intent on developing businesses from scratch. The day James turned 18 (three months after I did) in April 1994, we ran to Madison, Connecticut, Town Hall and filed our first DBA (doing business as) application. It was for Shore Marketing, a business we created to provide small businesses with marketing support, to publish restaurant guides and to help businesses with grand openings. (At one event, I wore a Teenage Mutant Ninja Turtle costume outside the grand opening of a new pizza restaurant on the day I was bound for UMass Amherst to begin my freshman year. My parents finally dragged me up to Amherst late in the afternoon.)

James and I seem to have the perfect balance of differences and things in common. It amazes me how much we can agree and disagree at the same time. Jim Theroux, my favorite professor from the School of Management at UMass, told me in no uncertain words that my partnership wouldn't last. He remains stunned when he hears we are "still together." But it works, and I suspect it is because of our differences. I am married with children. James is single. I am conservative, James less so. We contribute different perspectives and chart different courses to attain similar goals. We attack problems with different solutions. Sometimes two heads are better than one.

Naiveté and instinct motivated us to start a community newspaper in my sophomore year of college. I was working as an advertising sales rep at UMass' Daily Collegian, a free daily newspaper. James and I became intrigued by this free distribution model and we began to investigate if we could transplant it to Madison. Seemed simple enough: sell advertising, get news and photos, print, and mail.

Above: Ryan Duques and James Warner at the Daily Collegian at UMass Amherst putting together the second edition of the *The Source* in June 1996.

We began in earnest over our winter break. We had set up our "office" in James' parents' home and started selling advertising ("Hi, we're home from college. Would you like to buy an ad in our new newspaper, and can we have payment up front?") and asking people to write local news articles.

Much can be written about the start of our newspaper

venture, but we don't have time for that. Let's just say that the paper launched with great results. We quickly took the paper to a monthly publication, then started publishing biweekly and finally weekly. In all, we started 14 community weekly newspapers and acquired two, resulting in coverage that spanned two thirds of the Connecticut shoreline into Rhode Island.

We sold the profitable chain of papers to The Day Publishing Company in 2008. It was a great ending. Not only did we find the perfect buyer, an independent newspaper company owned by a non-profit trust, but we sold the company at its height. Plus, as an entrepreneur it was becoming too big. With 75 employees, layers of managers, and a board to report to, it had became difficult and slow-going to execute new strategies. Not what I live for. I had a long list of new ventures I wanted work on.

The Right Time to Start is Now

Executing a new business idea quickly can be difficult under any conditions. Most people I talk to about the business ideas they had but never did anything with use the "timing wasn't right" excuse. That drives me nuts; they have no idea what they are missing.

Probably the only time in my life that the timing was right was in college when we launched the newspapers. (My parents didn't agree. Through countless discussions they tried to dissuade me: College should be used for studying and fun, not starting newspapers back home.)

And the timing for this 37-day exercise couldn't have been more challenging.

First, my wife Erin and I have these two beautiful little girls. Analise is two-and-a-half and Alexandrine is seven months old. They demand a large portion of my attention and get it without protest. "Daddy, dress me up as a fairy." "Daddy, I want a snack." If I walk out of Alexandrine's sight, she cries. Sounds crazy, but I love every second.

My wife Erin with our two girls, Alexandrine and Analise.

Analise is full of energy. Alexandrine smiles constantly, loves to be held, and won't sleep through the night. My time with them is something I would have never imagined. But, as an entrepreneur who, in a previous life had the freedom to brainstorm whenever, travel whenever, have meetings whenever, these two little people have added a new challenge to the Big Plan. Plus, I haven't had a decent night's sleep in at least six months. Despite having an excellent partner in Erin, she is a busy attorney, and we both seem to have 10 balls in the air at any given time, but without a shred of doubt those two girls are our priority and greatest accomplishments.

Second, as a serial entrepreneur, I have three other major business ventures in various stages of startup in addition to the venture discussed in this book.

The first is four-year-old TutaPoint.com, which I founded with partner Michael Callaghan. This online education company provides live, online tutoring sessions and supplemental materials to students across the country. This business is a passion of mine but has been slow to develop. Ironically, during this 37-day period, we signed one of our largest tutoring contracts to date, providing tutoring services to more than 22,000 students—exciting, but time-consuming. Luckily, at TutaPoint I have a great team.

Then there's Interactive Digital, a Digital Out of Home network of digital-content screens fixed on top of gas pumps along southern Connecticut. The screens deliver useful content and local advertising to a captive audience (a marketer's dream!). James and I launched this niche business in early 2010 and have been encouraged by its growth, return on investment, and future opportunities in digital signage. Content for the screens comes from our local ABC News affiliate, and we sell sponsorships to businesses that can use audio and video to promote their business in 15-second slots.

A venture that would never qualify for this 37-day challenge is Sachem Bank, a project James and I founded in 2006 to bring a De Novo commercially oriented bank to our community. Over a four-year period, we rode out the financial meltdown and banking industry turmoil and attracted more than 30 like-minded local business leaders to organize the bank. We attained our temporary banking charter from the state Department of Banking and launched a capital campaign.

While this venture has provided amazing insight into banking and is unlike any other startup I have ever launched, it is a painfully slow and oftentimes very discouraging. Like every other project, the team of individuals we assembled to execute this project has been what's kept the project alive. As one of the only upstart banks in the nation, we have attracted a great deal of interest from those seeking a fresh bank charter, and I am optimistic that the project will result in a new community bank that will serve small business owners.

Energy deregulation in Connecticut allowed James and I to launch an energy marketing company in 2007 with our partner Tom LaTorre. This one's not a huge time consumer: the venture requires me to update a website, run reports, and advertise our rates online. The energy is provided by ConEdison Solutions, Inc. The company provides us with a small but consistent monthly revenue stream, which helps to cover our modest second-floor office space with big windows overlooking the main street of our hometown.

Finally, James and I own and operate a few websites. None of them are profitable, but, as we discovered during the 37 days, they do have something valuable: registered users. Not many, but enough.

Guidezilla.com is a hyper-local, event-calendar website. When we launched in 2006, James and I were minority partners, but a few years ago we bought out our partners. After a substantial redesign and efforts to generate revenue, the site has remained sleepy and maintains just a few thousand registered users. We continue to support the site with regular updates, Facebook integration, and Twitter updates, and while the users are dedicated, the site has never achieved our goals.

Finally, with hopes of navigating the complex regulatory rules of selling wine online, James and I bought the domain wineencyclopedia.com in 2006. We developed a site that allows users to rate and review wines and join a community of oenophiles. The site has attracted users, but we scuttled efforts to sell wine across state lines after endless research and legal review. Although we aren't sure exactly how the wine site fits into our future plans, we continue to invest small amounts in updates and content. You never know.

☞ **TOOLS USED:**

Samsung Epic Galaxy S 4G on Sprint: Allows me to access all of my e-mail accounts, websites, and phone calls from one fast mobile device. I love the large bright screen, and the pullout large keyboard was a must for me (although I have learned that typing on the screen isn't as bad as I expected).

HP Netbook: Coupled with my Verizon Wireless air card, I can access the Internet with this mini laptop anytime, anywhere allowing me to update websites, schedule email campaigns and manage TutaPoint servers.

I Run, But Not for Exercise.

Only rarely do I realize that I tend to run during the work day.

When I get to the office in the morning, I run up the back staircase.

I often dart from our office across Boston Post Road to the post office.

I run to and from my car.

I have no idea why I am compelled to run during business hours. It isn't for exercise, and I doubt I am capturing more than a few seconds of extra time. I think I run because I am excited. I can't wait to get to the next stop where I can allow my mind to release all the ideas that have been piling up since my last stop. I run fastest in the morning. After a night of sleep and a morning with my girls, my head is ready to explode with the ideas that have accumulated since the day before.

When this passion for business is in motion, I can hardly think of anything else. At the movies, I'm thinking of the venture. At dinner with family or friends: thinking about the venture. On vacation ... well you get the idea. I love it. I try my hardest not to be obsessed, but occasionally it happens. Just ask Erin.

At the start of 2011, I started running more frequently: James and I had another idea.

Start the Clock

I want every project to be brought to market as soon as possible. Like an enthusiastic gardener that keeps checking on her plants, I want my ventures to be born and grow quickly. Of course, not every new venture is meant to be brought to market with speed (Sachem Bank). And others are in fields that require years of foundation-building (TutaPoint.com). But every once in awhile, you come across an idea that can be launched almost immediately. The idea James and I came across not only could be brought to market quickly, it had to be.

Identifying a Niche

In early January 2011 James and I started discussing whether we should consider starting a daily deal website, similar to Groupon and LivingSocial for our market in Connecticut. Over the past few years we had established an unwritten rule of "no new projects," allowing only Interactive Digital to be added to our list of active ventures. Our time was already extremely fragmented between projects, so we couldn't allow ourselves to become overloaded, which would surely result in failures across the board.

But this idea was intriguing: a website, employing the full power of social media, search-engine optimization, and business connections to promote a business's deal for a day or two, sell vouchers, and split the revenue with the partner merchant. It seemed to require the skill sets and contacts James and I already had. We also had an additional and necessary resource: several thousand Guidezilla.com users in our market who already received a weekly e-mail from us.

What added to our excitement was the fact that the big national players had made very little, if any, attempt to penetrate our market, which is just outside New Haven, Connecticut, 90 miles east of Manhattan.

Over the next few days, James and I started texting about the idea and chatting over lunch. Our excitement grew, and soon we were ready to seriously investigate this business as a potential new venture.

Our Resources

From the beginning, it was easy for us to identify the synergies that Guidezilla and this new website could share. Both ventures focused on events in a geographic region that were marketed to registered users via e-mail and social networks. This was our starting point.

Within an hour of deciding to pursue this venture, we constructed a very simple e-mail survey using the widely popular Constant Contact and sent it to our Guidezilla membership. Respondents to the survey were entered into a drawing for a Starbucks gift card. (Congratulations Geoff C!)

Before lunchtime we had results and they were clear: 89% of the respondents said they would or might be interested in receiving regular deals from local merchants and restaurants from us. Just 21% of our respondents had purchased a deal from one of the giants, which reassured us that Groupon had not yet made meaningful penetration in our market. (This was just before Groupon's controversial Tibetan Super Bowl ad aired.)

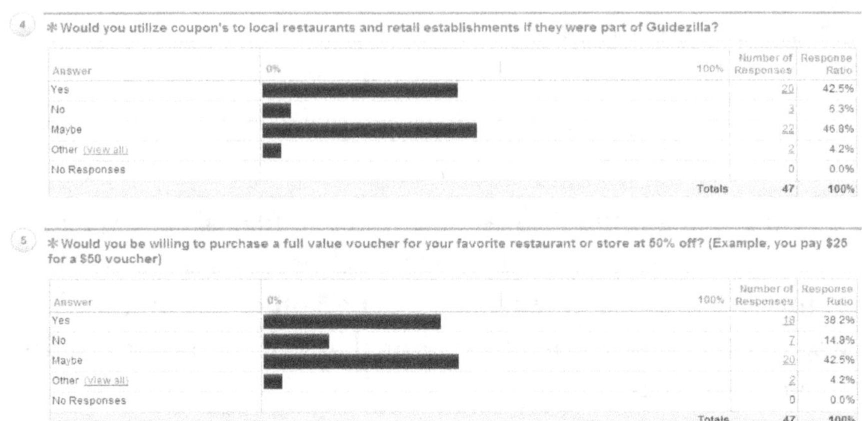

Guidezilla users responding that they would be interested in a local deals website.

Above: 21 % of users indicate they have purchased coupons from one of the giants.

☞ TOOLS USED:

Constant Contact: Excellent e-mail marketing service, which also (for an extra fee) allows you to build and deploy quick surveys. You can get results in minutes. Perfect when you don't have much time to get the thoughts of constituents.

Planning the Site

From a technical and speed-to-market perspective, it seemed best to make this site part of Guidezilla.com. I was pretty adamant that we wouldn't want to develop and build an entirely new brand and site to facilitate the daily deals. James wasn't as convinced of that as I was, but he went along with the plan to leverage the Guidezilla brand and site. He was concerned that the name, look, and feel weren't exactly what we were looking for.

By early afternoon we were working out how to integrate this venture with Guidezilla.

One tiny hurdle is that neither James nor I have any meaningful website coding experience. I know enough HTML to update text or add a photo, but any attempts beyond that usually result in a call to the webmaster to "please, please fix the page." We both seem to have a good sense of what "can" be done, although our expectations and the programmer's estimates on how long coding will take often deviate (greatly).

Over the past five years I have found a number of accomplished programmers using the website Elance.com. The site allows users to post projects in need of staff, and providers with those skills bid on them. You can see a provider's work histories and reviews from people that have used that provider in the past. I discovered a great company based in India that I have used more and more over the past four years for TutaPoint. The company now provides all of the development and technical support needs for the website, and the programmers and managers have become friends, even though they are nine time zones away.

Just after a lunch meeting on day 1, I typed up a scope of

work (an outline of features we wanted to see on the website). I wanted to bring a daily deal to the Guidezilla.com website, e-mail it to our users, provide full administrative back-end support, and easily integrate everything into social networks. James and I reviewed and refined the document a few times and then I posted it to the team in India for their thoughts and cost estimates.

Here was the scope of work I sent to Rahul Mehta, the principle of my preferred web programming company.

1. Ability for ADMIN to post new deals (Can be more than one)

    a. UPLOAD OF DEAL: Allow admin only to upload content for deal (photo, title, description text, email text, value, price, discount, address, total deals needed to purchase before deal is active (for example, 10 coupons need to be sold before the deal is active, see Groupon for example), expiration date and activation date, which is when it goes live (live date) on site and admin email (for access and reports to be sent)

        i. Additionally, allow admin to list the zip codes the deal is shown on the website for and which emails. Can select specific zip codes, radius from a zip code or all network

        ii. Ability for Admin to automatically create Google Ads for this coupon (is this possible?)

    b. WEEKLY EMAILS: Weekly GZ emails will include text as entered by Admin at the TOP of each weekly email for the deals in that zip code (radius or all)… you will note that this functionality is already in place for the email sponsorship function… so leveraging this existing code should be simple.

c. SPONSOR PORTAL: For each coupon campaign that is created, a simple ADMIN portal is automatically created, username and URL sent via email as soon as campaign goes live (live date), which allows the sponsor of the coupon deal the ability to log-in and track how many people have purchased their deal, get reports and ability to mark COUPON USED. Simple search would allow admin to search by name, coupon code. Also would allow them to email a report.

d. CANCEL DEAL: ADMIN will have ability to cancel any deal or change terms, content, etc.

e. ADMIN report by deal (by campaign), also by date, etc to get payment information, total sold, etc. Also, need to get transaction reports by customer.

f. Allow users to store a credit card on file

2. Add Ability to allow users to purchase a coupon discount on Guidezilla

a. To view coupon user will need to sign in using existing database or create account. We would like this to pop open in Modal window as soon as they click "See This Week's Deals" unless they are already logged in. Allow users to log in via Facebook connect and also so they can see who their friends are that are using the deals too… see example of this on LivingSocial.com. Users must be a GZ user to access and purchase coupons.

b. Users can view discount coupon page with deal listings (See Attachment A). This is very similar layout to existing guidezilla event list page, but must be logged in.

c. When user clicks on deal, they are taken to the deal details page (see attachment B). This is very similar to existing event details page

d. Also on this page there is YELP rating and details in box from YELP API (http://www.yelp.com/developers/documentation) to show our users what others are saying about the establishment. If no Yelp data exists, then this does not appear.

e. User can view deal from this page… Share the deal via existing Social Network apps (already being used on GZ) and also press Buy or Gift this deal.

    i. If they buy it, they will purchase the coupon and will need to enter their credit card information (this will use GZ existing PayPal API for billing)

        1. Once they purchase coupon, they will be taken to a page where they can print the deal. Additionally, this deal will be available in their My Deals from their My Account, so they can reprint the deal if they lose it.

        2. There is also a Modal box that opens on this page that says Share This Deal Now, If 25 People Don't Use This Deal It Is Not Activated!" and the Share app

        3. Each Coupon print out or when viewed online will have a unique

CODE (number and letters as well as a QR-Code).

    ii. If they Gift the Discount, the same functions happen, except after payment they are asked if they want to print the certificate or email it to the recipient… if they want to email, they will be asked to enter the recipients information. Again, this will be saved in the My Deals page so they can reprint or re-email.

3. We want on My Account… a page called My Coupon Queue, which shows their coupons (users coupons)… whether they have been redeemed yet, etc. They can also request refund… this refund will request refund through PayPal API and also send email to merchant that coupon is now VOID. If coupon has already been redeemed or offer is no longer being offered (end date) this option for refund is not available.

4. IMPORTANT ELEMENTS

    a. Sharing on social media websites is a KEY element, so pages must be easily designed for sharing on facebook so that text and photo comes through properly

    b. Remove the texting option from all pages (this no longer works) and replace with Deal of the Week image ad which takes user to www.guidezilla.com/deals

    c. Pages are LOCATION sensitive similar to the rest of Guidezilla, so users will only see deals in that area if ADMIN lists them for that zip code, radius or all area.

    d. The Deals page will have This Weeks Deals… Last

> Week's Deals and Old Deals all listed Pages need
> to be well optimized for SEO (can we get Google
> Around the log-in so the search engine can see the
> Deals pages?)

Day 1 was productive. We had conducted meaningful research, analyzed the results, determined a platform, produced a scope of work, and started to develop a timeline for launch.

That night, I brought the scope of work home and tried to describe the plan to Erin between dinner, PJ time with the girls, and bedtime stories. I fell asleep excited.

At 5 a.m. on day 2 I received the quote from Rahul. To produce the necessary site enhancements it would take about two weeks and cost about $2,000. Reasonable, I thought. But there was a small hiccup, according to Rahul. Guidezilla.com was written in the now antiquated language of ASP. Rahul only has one programmer who is proficient in coding this language, so this would need to be a side project for that programmer. It was also Republic Day in India, which meant a long holiday weekend, so there would be no work on the site for almost a week.

With that in mind, I was pretty sure the project wouldn't be finished in two weeks; it would likely take double that time. But still, four weeks wasn't bad, and we needed that time to prepare for the launch.

By 9 a.m. my brain was just about bursting with all of the things I wanted to do that day. I drove my car a little faster on my one-mile commute and ran up the stairs to my office.

I started setting up meetings with people I knew would be integral to the launch. My first e-mail was to veteran local news anchor and friend Ann Nyberg. Ann, who has been on the air for more than 20 years, is a social media expert and has built a significant following of local people who enjoy her story-telling and nose for news about local people and places. She has reached Facebook's maximum of 5,000 friends and recently launched a new website, NetworkConnecticut.com.

Ann, who lives in my extended neighborhood, gave me an on-the-air confidence boost when I was 20 years old, when her station ran a segment about one of our newest newspapers. As she sat behind the anchor desk looking impressed she said, "These two are on the right track."

Ann responded in four minutes (she must have been busy that morning), and we quickly set up a coffee meeting.

Next, I e-mailed via Facebook two enterprising young women whom I met through Ann. Maggie and Sara impressed me last fall when we met to discuss daily video news clips for newspaper websites. They had a large following and I thought perhaps we could involve video in the site. They responded and we had a meeting set.

I had met Sara and Maggie once before at a coffee shop in Middletown. We agreed to meet at that location again, and this time James came along to help us determine how we might fit their talents into the plan.

It is not important to mention (but I will anyway) that Maggie and Sara are in their early twenties and both have been crowned winners in beauty pageants. Now, I do not know many beauty queens, but I can tell you that these two do not fit your typical stereotype. They've got it. They had an open mind, had good instincts, and, best of all, thought we had a good idea.

Above: Sara O'Leary and Maggie Slysz.

James and I pitched a simple concept: they would produce short videos for select deals. These 15- to 30-second deals would be placed on Facebook, YouTube, and on SavingsClique. Additionally, we would use the videos to advertise the deals and promote SavingsClique across our IDTV network of screens at the gas stations. For each video they produced, they would receive a small piece of the revenue generated from that deal. This would encourage them to share the videos (and the deals) with people in their networks.

This also would help to differentiate SavingsClique from some of the other daily-deal websites. We would put a face on the deal. These two young women would put some personality behind our deal—something the other websites don't do.

They were excited, we were excited. Perfect.

Editorial content about each deal was necessary. Before a visitor to the site decided to purchase one of these deals from us, they needed to be sold. The words describing the partner merchant and the offer needed to be professionally written and error-free.

James is one of the worst spellers I have ever come across. I can say this because I am only a little bit better. We can laugh about this now because we no longer own the newspapers. I mean, how can two of the worst spellers start and operate a chain of successful (and mostly error-free) newspapers? Good editors. Luckily I've maintained contact with all of them, and they remain more than happy to write some freelance copy on the side. We engaged our writers to pen short articles about each partner merchant, using details about the business from the business's website and from information posted about them on the web. Add in some verbiage about the deal of the day, and voila!—a professional editorial piece that made us and the merchant look good. Then we sent the articles along to Sara and Maggie for them to use in their videos: one message across two media.

One of my editorial contacts, Marisa Nadolny, first came to my office at the newspaper when I was 20-something years old. We needed a part-time afternoon receptionist/copy editor/writer and she needed a foot in the door at a newspaper. She had just graduated from UConn with a degree in English. She seemed nice enough and actually arrived on time for the interview. I hired her.

Marisa rose through the ranks at the newspapers, eventually becoming one of my best editors. She outlived my tenure at the company and still writes for the company. After I left I brought Marisa in to work on my side projects. She wrote and edited most of the original text on the TutaPoint.com website and edited two math books. If you check the cover of this book, chances are, Marisa is the editor.

Meanwhile, James, who was much more familiar with Groupon and LivingSocial, forwarded me a slew of deals from the giants. Clothing. Restaurants. Spas. Oil changes. Some performed well, others didn't. We took note.

Back to Ann Nyberg: I met with Ann for two reasons. First, I wanted an honest opinion. Second, I was hoping to somehow bring her into the venture, allowing her to do what she does best: tell stories and promote local businesses.

Ann Nyberg's NetworkConnecticut.com.

We usually meet at Starbucks. More caffeine. I brought a few sketches of the idea to show to her. She gave it to me straight: she loved the idea, but didn't love integrating it with Guidezilla. Why? A purple monster (our Guidezilla logo and mascot) won't play well to a female audience, something that she thought was critical. She also felt the site needed its own identity. James had been saying something similar for a few days. I had protested this strategy for one main reason: I was worried about the additional technical requirements this would involve—a new website, database, secure credit card processing, etc, etc. etc. My head hurt.

In hindsight, technical roadblocks (or any roadblock) aren't reasons to not do what your gut tells you is the right thing to do. (This book could have been called "32 Days to Launch.")

Site development was slow-going, and my requests for updates and demo screens weren't being accommodated quickly. This made me nervous, so I reached out to Rahul who said that the programmer's father had become ill, but he expected him to return quickly. Not good.

> **☞ TOOLS USED:**
>
> **Friends that can edit:** No matter what business venture I find myself in, having someone close by that can edit the written word is invaluable. A user's first impression of our website (and our brand) is gained from the words they read.
>
> **Starbucks:** Excellent place to meet, and they now offer free Wi-fi.
>
> **Rolodex:** Keep it handy.

Change of Plans

James and I discussed what we had learned over the past week. We needed to change course. At this point, we agreed that the challenges of working within the Guidezilla framework were limiting us and would not ultimately create the unique identity we needed.

Rahul and I spoke about other options. He recommended building a separate site using the updated ASP.Net language, which would allow us to pull data and run transactions through the Guidezilla databases. This solved one big concern, which was recreating an entirely new back-end.

James started working with a few designers who would create the site's "wire frame" pages that we would lay on top of the code.

Rahul had a team of 20 ASP.Net programmers he could deploy on this code to meet the deadline.

This seemed like a good course of action. Separate identity, better platform, and we would make the deadline. I slept that night.

An Easier Way?

During James' programming research, he came across a company that offered an off-the-shelf, daily-deal website package. The customer throws a brand and URL on the site, pays a fee, and uses the software solution instead of building their own. My immediate reaction: no way. To allow someone else to control the site's code was to give up our ability to control the customer's experience. Bad idea. Besides, Rahul was already working on it.

Later that day I watched some of the videos from this website. Huh. It was pretty good. Seemed to have all of the bells and whistles we wanted and it promised tech support. Plus it offered a 60-day money-back guarantee.

By the end of the day I conceded to James that maybe we should use that solution.

It's all In a Name

Because we had decided to pull the website out of Guidezilla we were faced with an unexpected task: choosing a name and URL. As much as I love marketing, the task of choosing a name and finding a URL is painful. Having struggled to name two little girls in recent years, the two experiences aren't dissimilar. This is a name that is going to stick with them (and this website) forever. Will my family like the name? Will friends make fun of it? A name says a lot. Pressure.

James and I had numerous brainstorming sessions. We asked friends who gave suggestions like dailysavings.com and save.com (thanks, but those are probably taken). We used thesauruses and translators (I thought a foreign name might be classy).

"Today at 3:30 we are picking a name, so come back to this table with your best ideas," I said to James on a Friday afternoon. We both came with a list of ideas. They all sucked.

Over that weekend we must have texted each other 100 times with ideas. I came up with redclique.com. I figured the word "red" was short and related to red-tag sale items in stores. "Clique" is an exclusive group, plus it sounds like "click" which is what you do with your mouse. James shot back "savingsclique.com."

On Monday we went back to our Guidezilla users with a list of site names to vote on. The results were very clear: the name would be SavingsClique.com. One respondent didn't like any name that included the word "clique." They said it meant "exclusive." Perfect. That was just what we wanted.

> **☞ TOOLS USED:**
>
> **NetworkSolutions.com:** Great site that allows visitors to type in a bunch of name ideas into a URL search tool. Unfortunately, most I searched for were taken.
>
> **NameStation.com:** Domain-name-generating website. Fun site that you can (and I did) spend hours on coming up with unique names.
>
> **Thesauraus.com:** Great site for finding words that mean "deal" or "offer." Another great site for generating ideas.
>
> **Translate.google.com:** Translate an English word into any language. This can be a fun exercise to see if a common English word might sound better in say, Italian. Plus, sometimes common English words are taken as URLs, but not their Italian or French counterpart.

Creating a Look

I thought the pain of developing a new brand was over with the name selection. I was wrong. I volunteered to work with designers to create the logo. Using local designers, someone I can sit with an describe my needs is usually my preference, but we had limited time and I was working on this in the middle of the night, so I used Elance.com to get our logo produced quickly.

Posting a logo project to Elance results in many bids from around the world. Weeding through them and choosing a designer is a challenge. After a point, all the portfolios start to look the same.

We wanted a logo that was fun and was synergistic with Guidezilla, since we thought there would still be some connection between the two sites. Additionally we wanted the designers to review the other major daily deal sites to gather some ideas.

This is what we posted to Elance:

"Our group is launching a new website similar to group deal sites like Groupon.com and LivingSocial.com.

"We seek a unique, classy, clean logo that incorporates our name (SavingsClique.com). We also seek a mascot concept and a few images.

"Time is important with this project."

The logos came back within 24 hours, but none of them really did it for us. In fact, some just looked silly. I tried to impress upon the designers our goals, continuously asking them to come up with something closer to Guidezilla. Here are the first round of logos we received back:

We tried to convey our desires with these e-mails:

February 3

1. Please read note below regarding our idea of a concept: We are seeking a CLEAN, easy to read logo... We were thinking of at least looking at one concept that used the $ as the S in SavingsClique.com We like logos that look raised (3-D) a little bit, but not drastic. This site is modeled after Groupon. com and LivingSocial.com, so you can get a feel for them...

2. We do not like the use of the tree / leaves, etc as this has nothing to do with our website... the website is a daily coupon website that offers money saving deals.

3. Of the logos sent, the manager would like to see a few additional versions of #4, with the .com below the logo and a few different fonts. Also, a couple with red top and a couple with blue top as you can see our site has blue here:

www.savingsclique.com

I hope you can send along additional concepts soon as we are hoping to finish project today.

Ryan

February 4

Shawn,

Thank you for the revised options.... again, can they also do a version as described below:

1. Please read note below regarding our idea of a concept: We are seeking a CLEAN, easy to read logo... We were thinking of at least looking at one concept that used the $ as the S in SavingsClique.com We like logos that look raised (3-D) a little bit, but not drastic. This site is modeled after Groupon. com and LivingSocial.com, so you can get a feel for them.

February 7

Hello,

We like the top logo on option 13. Can you please see green color on www. savingsclique.com and change the red to that green... Also, can you send one reverse logo too with black background, green top and white letters, since this logo will be sitting where that current draft sits now?

Ryan

February 7

Also,

I am sorry, I made a mistake, it is the bottom one on option 13.

Also, I am requesting that an additional concept is created similar to our logo at Guidezilla.com with the $ sign... we like how the Guidezilla logo is 3-dimensional. For this we would want the logo to be green (match site www. savingsclique.com), black, yellow and red are all okay to use. You can find the Guidezilla logo at www.guidezilla.com

Ryan

February 9

Sarah,

Option 19 is the one we want... can we see a couple more just like it? We would like the following also:

1. The word "Clique" to be black - for the reverse logo (on black background) the word "Clique" should be silver.

2. The Word savings in a brighter red (for one variation spec)

3. Both words to be "glossy" looking and to be puffy looking, similar to how guidezilla.com logo is in all future versions.

We are almost there! Hope we can complete and release funds today!

Ryan

February 10

Sarah,

Thank you.

We like option 23 - can you send it as is, but also on a white background? Also, can you send as just JPG as SQUARE image 2x2 for use on facebook? To do this, put Savings on one line and Clique.com on the second line. Okay?

Ryan

Finally we chose a logo. Partially out of exhaustion and necessity, and a little because we liked it:

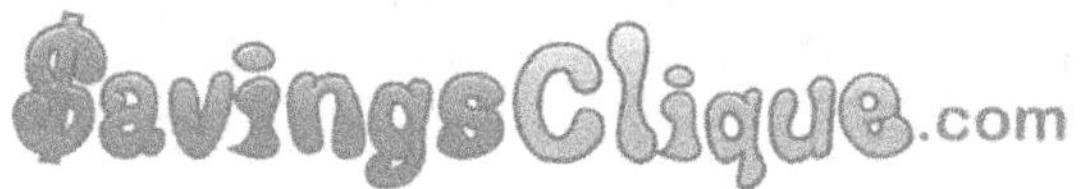

Having friends with various skill sets are important (especially when you aren't really an expert in anything yourself). Elise Hergan is an accomplished architect and designer and has been a friend since high school. As one of my closest friends, I know she'll give me unfiltered advice. While none of our options caught Elise's attention, she provided excellent feedback (that we will likely use when we redesign the logo).

Within a few days of our choice, we knew we would be updating the logo sooner rather than later. Punishment for settling.

☞ TOOLS USED:

Elance.com: Finding a quick and cheap graphic designer is a sure thing, but sometimes the responses to your project are overwhelming and time-consuming to go through.

Rolodex: Call on friends with different skill sets as you are in each stage of development. Ask for their honest opinion and be open to change. It is a lot easier to make changes now than it will be after launch. Also, keep a list of local designers handy as you will need professionally designed collateral throughout the life of your business. While you can always use Elance.com as a backup, it is much easier (yet sometimes more expensive) to sit down with a designer in person to describe your needs.

Change of Provider

A week into preparing the off-the-shelf site for our needs, we started encountering some roadblocks. It now appeared that the site didn't have functionality James and I consider essential.

Additionally we were disappointed with the response of the company's self-proclaimed "top-notch" customer service. The most common response to our request was "that is scheduled for future development." What did that mean? It meant the site doesn't do that and won't anytime soon.

James approached them with a last-ditch e-mail to determine if they could meet our essential items:

TO: Daily Deal Website Vendor

FROM: SavingsClique.com

A. Something that will be upgraded at a later time (and give an ETA)

B. Something we set up incorrectly

C. Not included in the daily deal website

1. Multiple deals showing on the sidebar example: Groupon.com and getmyperks.com

2. First time visit Login screen is clean and shows a deal behind the request of email address and then never comes back again once they have signed up. Example: doubletakedeals.com

3. Auto login via facebook account which remembers you when you log back onto site and link showing how many of your friends are also using the site...would be cool to have the Facebook pic up there also. Example: Groupon.com and livingsocial.com

4. Users have a tab in their profile page to save their credit card info so they can auto checkout without reentering their payment info over and over again. Exp: Groupon and livingsocial

5. Emails that when item is shared the pictures and offer are clean and simple. Exp. groupon and livingsocial

6. A separate marketing area on the site for the potential business. Exp: http://www.howperksworks.com

7. The ability to set a coupon up and send a proof (PDF or web) of the actual offer and printed coupon to the advertiser to approve before it is set in the system. Kind of like a pending offer tab that only the advertisers and the admin has access to.

8. Reports. Basically we are looking for ways to easily report on the individual deals, monthly results, number of sign ups broken down in multiple ways etc. Maybe they are there but we didn't see them yet.

9. There needs to be some level of control in the comments area... either the admin can delete comments after a user reports as "inappropriate" or some kind of control that needs approval process.

10. Affiliate tracking on a referral basis. Both for partner websites to get "credit" for referral and for users to refer friends to get rewards like $10 in their account for getting other people to sign up. Exp: Groupon at the top of a logged in account.

Many elements are similar to existing event details page.

Numbers at the top will not be images, instead they will contain numbers generated from the ADMIN and they are:

1. FULL VALUE

    $##

2. GUIDEZILLA PRICE

    $##

3. DISCOUNT

    ##% (calculate by dividing guidezilla price by full price)

4. DAYS REMAINING

    \#   (calculate by today's date – end date)

5. BOUGHT SO FAR

    \#\#

It Pays to Reconnect

I had been e-mailing Polly Kreisman, who operates the successful hyper-local news site theloopny.com. Over the past couple of years Polly and I had been discussing how we could possibly integrate the Guidezilla calendar feed into her community events listings. She had recently released a new version of her site and was showing me around.

I told Polly how James and I were working on a deals website as an offshoot of Guidezilla. I asked if she might be interested in working together down the road to bring deals to her site. That's when she showed me her deals portal "Loopon." She already had a platform provider, Dealicio.com, and it looked good. After she gave me a rundown of how the site works (including fees), she provided me with the name of her contact.

On the surface, Dealicio.com seemed to have the essential features we needed. I sent an e-mail to the contact person and went into James' office with the news of a potential new provider.

James' response to the idea was lukewarm. He had already invested a week of his time learning how to use the website we had selected. He had sat through webinars, drafted and responded to countless e-mails, and started entering our information into the platform. I understood his initial resistance, but the existing site and its features sucked.

Finally, on a Friday afternoon James and I developed a list of the items we considered essential. There were 10 items. We sent a prioritized list to the developers and asked for an immediate response.

Monday morning rolled around and we hadn't received a response. Eager to know the fate of the project, James called one of the principal of the company who indicated he hadn't seen the list. Not a good sign. James had to submit it to the "other" support ticket system.

Finally they responded. "Future development"; "No"; "Not available."

No-go.

It didn't take us long to decide that we had to make a move. We didn't have many options.

One possibility was to revert back to our plan to develop the site ourselves. In many ways this seemed most promising. At completion we would own the site and have complete control over its functionality and features. However, as we got deeper into the project, I started realizing just how robust these sites were. The endless features, complex databases, transaction processing needs, API connections to e-mail services, etc. My head started to hurt when I considered the amount of coding that would need to be done. Then there's the testing phase; the site would need to operate glitch-free, or we would quickly jeopardize our reputation over the social media networks.

Then I spoke to Graham Clark, Polly's guy at Dealicio. I was impressed by what I heard. Dealicio had been working with radio stations for years to develop similar deal websites. The site was feature-rich, too. Although there were no large upfront fees to pay, the site would take a percentage of the revenue we generate.

While we weren't excited about the prospect of sharing each dollar we earned, James was eager to get a conference call with Graham.

Graham returned to his office at 5 p.m. and we started the call. It went on and on. I had agreed to go to the grocery store before going home, so there I was still on the call in the produce aisle. At the checkout. And eventually as I fed Analise dinner.

While Analise started demanding a chocolate cookie for dessert we hit a major roadblock. The minimum sales thresholds that Graham quoted seemed unattainable. It seemed impossible to ramp up to sell the amount of deals necessary to meet the minimum monthly sales requirement.

It was time for Graham to sell us. Graham: we are experienced entrepreneurs who successfully started 16 newspapers and acquired two before selling the profitable company. We understand the local media market, we have a user base, and we have a network of people in social media. I'm guessing he Googled us to verify we weren't making it up. I would have.

I knew we passed Graham's test when he said, "You can understand that I need to flush out the guy that thinks it would be a good idea to start a deal website because he just lost his job." While I feel for those who are unemployed (and believe with the right passion and contacts they would be as or even more successful than me and James), I understood Graham's point. He couldn't afford to invest his time and money into building and supporting a deal site for us unless he knew it would produce revenue for him too.

We determined that an agreement with a ramp-up period would work for both parties.

The result of the two-plus-hour call was promising. We asked Graham to put together an agreement for our review and to get his team prepared to bring us on-board. I slept better that night.

Meanwhile, James couldn't wait to call the other platform and request our no-questions-asked refund. He did that the next morning and began the process of preparing the Dealicio platform for SavingsClique.

> ☞ **TOOLS USED:**
>
> **Rolodex:** Reconnecting with people you've done business with or meet with socially regularly is a must for any entrepreneur. You never know what they might be working on or who they can connect you to.

Developing a Facebook Presence

Daily deal websites depend on social media traffic. These sites would not be nearly as successful without Facebook, Twitter, etc., so as soon as we had a logo, we built our Facebook page. Recent changes at Facebook enable businesses to create unique pages. James had seen some of the daily deal websites utilizing "custom tabs" on their Facebook pages, so I investigated how to add this to our Facebook page. Within a few hours I turned to Elance and I posted the following:

"SavingsClique.com requests a programmer to work in the newly launched Facebook for business fan page to create default landing page that displays 'invite your friends,' with a custom image at top with an arrow inviting user to 'Like Us' very similar to this Facebook landing page: http://www.facebook.com/groupon

"This page uses the new design, launched this month, so programmer MUST be familiar with new Facebook design and development.

"Must have ability to create graphics using our logo for this page. In bid, show pages you have created on Facebook and give us examples of how we can create our Facebook page to generate 'likes.'"

Above: After the user clicks the "like" button, the arrow and film are removed and the user is free to explore the custom-built page.

We selected Nizam within a day because he provided excellent samples. He got right to work programming a custom welcome page for our SavingsClique page. This was cool. The first time a visitor comes to our Facebook page they see a custom graphic with our logo, YouTube video, and links to our current deals. But the part I loved the best was that for people who hadn't "liked" our page yet, there was a semitransparent overlay arrow pointing to the Facebook "like" button at the top of the page. Once the user clicks "like," the overlay is removed and they can see our page.

TOOLS USED:

Google.com: Research how to create custom Facebook tabs

http://developers.facebook.com: Research creating custom tabs on their developer website

Elance.com: Hired programmer "Salsoftreal" (Nizam) to construct custom code

Getting Deals, the Learning Curve

All this technical stuff, but what about the stuff that actually makes a daily deal business work? I believe there are three main ingredients:

1. A trustworthy, professional website and brand

2. A user base of people to whom you will send the deals

3. Deals people actually want to buy

We have spent the entire book so far talking about the first ingredient. Very important, but without the other two, we will be dead in the water.

First, we worked to engage our Guidezilla members to participate in this additional service. From the beginning we knew this base of users would be our initial catalyst to spread the word on the deals. One little hurdle was the change in brand. One advantage of the original concept to make the deal site part of Guidezilla was the ability to run the deals and its promotion through our existing brand. But, we didn't want to confuse, or worse, upset our Guidezilla members when they received an e-mail from SavingsClique. So, we made sure the members knew it was coming by placing ads on Guidezilla touting the arrival of Guidezilla's new "sister site." Additionally we e-mailed members with the news and the survey results and thanked them for selecting the name. To respect users who were outside the geographic area of the deals, we also scrubbed this list by zip code.

This avoided some, but not all, of the confusion we aimed to avoid—more on this later.

A daily deals website is dependent on thousands of viewers.

Expecting an overnight success with our mere database of a few thousand people would be silly. We had to develop an aggressive (my opinion anyway) online advertising program. To do this I researched key words buying for Google, Bing, and Yahoo, and I prepared extensive Facebook advertising.

I was familiar with Adwords by Google. I already had an account, which I had been using for years for TutaPoint.com and Collective Energy. Google Adwords is fun to use and integrates well into Google Analytics.

Facebook is another advertising platform with which I am familiar. This one is even more fun than Adwords (yes, I'm a bit of a marketing geek). You can drill down demographically, geographically, and by interest, groups, etc. to show your ads to your target audience.

I did not have any experience advertising on Yahoo or Bing. I went to Yahoo.com and clicked on the "Small Business Solutions" link on the bottom of the home page. I was delighted to learn that I would be able to create ads for both Yahoo and Bing from this one account. Perfect, a time-saver! I spent a few minutes filling out the account creation form, pressed "create account," and... UGH! "Thanks for contacting us, a sales representative will call you soon." No! I didn't want to talk to a sales rep, I wanted to run ads... i.e. give them money. And guess what? As of this writing, I have never received a call from a Yahoo sales rep. No ads on Yahoo and Bing. Oh well.

James had been cataloging (along with purchasing a few) deals from other areas of Connecticut and Boston for a few weeks. We were starting to get a good feel for the deals that work (restaurants, massages, spas) and those that don't (teeth whitening).

Now it was time to pitch the concept to local merchants. Thankfully, our Rolodexes are pretty extensive. In addition to being co-publishers of the area's community newspapers for 13 years, James is the former vice president of the Guilford Chamber of Commerce and I'm a former president of the Madison Chamber of Commerce. I also sit on the Madison Economic Development Commission. Plus, we grew up here. We know a few local business owners.

Unlike the newspaper business, these restaurants, merchants, and service providers would be partners, not customers. We needed to align our brand with popular, respected businesses. Our success would be tied directly to how our users and the community responded the deals we presented. This took a little getting used to.

James has maintained a great relationship with one of the area's most well established, multi-generational businesses: Bishop's Orchards. In addition to their famous apple orchard, the Bishops have grown their Guilford, Connecticut, business into an impressive niche grocery store. This would be a perfect first deal. It would generate excitement and create instant credibility for our SavingsClique brand.

Convincing the Bishop's people that it was in their best interest to offer a $20 voucher for $10, and then split the profits, was difficult. After all, Bishop's had been around since the 1871. They have an extensive marketing program (including the use of our IDTV network, thank you!), and thousands and thousands of customers. So why would they need to throw a deal out there?

James worked like mad to explain the benefits of being our first deal. First, they would receive a huge amount of online advertising on Google and Facebook (not Yahoo). This would give Bishop's a big branding push. Plus, it would likely bring some new or infrequent customers into the market.

Finally, after some tough negotiating between James and Sarah

Bishop DellaVentura, Bishop's agreed to be our lead deal. A major coup. Nice work James.

What followed were numerous conversations with other merchants and restaurants that we wanted to get in the queue. Businesses that we respected, products and services we would buy.

It was great to walk into a business and not sell something. We really were seeking partners. Most of the conversations started with an overview of how the deal works. I was teaching these veteran business owners about an entirely new way to promote their businesses. It was a pay-for-performance model. No cost or fees upfront. The more successful a deal is, the more services or product they provide at a discount. That is their liability. If a business understands their cost to acquire a new customer, they get this program. More important, if they understand how to convert a new customer into an engaged, long-term customer, they understand the true power of this program.

Red Tomato is my favorite Madison pizzeria. Perfect thin crust pizza. My regular visits have made the owner, Chuck, a friend. Despite the fact that Chuck had always respectfully declined to advertise in the newspaper, I called on him one morning while he was making the dough for the day. His hands covered in dough, he seemed intrigued by the concept. One problem, he literally couldn't fit any more pies into the ovens on Friday and Saturday nights, so providing a discount would erode profits and nothing else. So we decided to craft a deal at a 53% discount for the days during the week that the ovens weren't (not yet anyway) at capacity.

Next I called on my favorite fish market, Star Fish Market in Guilford. Mike and Colette seemed equally intrigued. Mike asked excellent questions (How do I book the revenue? What happens to the voucher after it expires? How do I track it?). Some I had answers to, many others I did not. Part of the advantage of going to friends first was to work out the kinks. After several rounds of questions and answers, Mike and Colette still weren't convinced that this type of promotion was right for their fish market, as they never offer discounts. They agreed to reassess after we launched the site. Certainly not a shut-down no.

I sent about a dozen e-mails over the next week to friends that owned bookstores, restaurants, tea stores, clothing stores, and massage therapy studios. They all greeted the concept with interest.

This was a great test: floating the concept to a wide cross-section of trusted business acquaintances. These are the kind of people that wouldn't be shy to tell me the idea sucks or that they would never ever do this. Their positive interest provided reinforcement that we were on the right track.

Back at the office James and I finalized the timeline for roll-out. We would launch on Wednesday, Feb. 16, with Bishop's. This deal would be followed on Friday, Feb. 18, by La Cuisine, a great restaurant for breakfast and prepared foods in Branford. James had negotiated this deal with the owners, also friends of ours. They too worried about their overflowing dining room on the weekends and asked that we restrict the deal to weekdays.

Because Bishop's didn't want their most frequent customers to be the only ones taking advantage of such a deep discount, they decided not to share their deal with their few thousand Facebook followers. However, they did agree to send out a note post-deal to thank those who purchased the deal and let their followers know about the La Cuisine deal. Perfect.

My first two deals would follow La Cuisine. Sound Body Therapeutic Massage is owned by Deb Cieri-Munster, a friend since we launched the newspapers in 1996. Deb and her staff give unbelievable massages and I knew her deal ($40 for an $80 massage) would be a hit. Following her deal we would feature Red Tomato Pizza.

Things were falling into place.

James and I delegated a few remaining items between ourselves. Thank goodness we were launching the site in a few days—we were getting anxious.

☞ TOOLS USED:

Rolodex: Call on friends and acquaintances (as well as businesses you are good customers at) to run your idea by. They will take your call and likely provide excellent feedback. Listen to them, they will be your customers!

Groupon, LivingSocial, NewEnglandPerks: To research which deals were popular and which were not.

Preparing for Launch

The Monday of launch week I met with Ann Nyberg again. I wanted her to participate as much as she could. For months I had been helping Ann brainstorm ways to generate revenue for her website NetworkConnecticut.com, and I thought an affiliate relationship could be one answer.

Over coffee at Starbucks Ann relayed that becoming an affiliate partner would likely violate her contract with her television station employer. However, she was eager to write the story about our newest venture for her website, and she wanted the story to break the day of our launch. So we scheduled an interview for the following day at the Guilford Diner.

James met with Ed Bartlett, owner of the popular shoreline entertainment website, shorelineoutandabout.com. Ed, who is seeking ways to monetize his site, was willing to sign up as an affiliate. For users that came to our site from his and bought a deal, he would receive compensation. It was a great deal for Ed and us and would introduce our deals to thousands of additional people.

Ed Bartlett's Shorelineoutandabout.com became a partner of SavingsClique.com.

A day before the launch we unceremoniously released our Facebook page. We did start encouraging Facebook friends of ours to like us, pushing to get to the necessary 25 "likes" to attain the coveted custom URL of facebook.com/savingsclique. As soon as Ann put it out there on her status, we shot from 20 likes to more than 65 and we got our custom URL. That girl has clout.

SavingsClique.com was featured on Ann Nyberg's NetworkConnecticut.com.

Everything was in place for the launch. The deal for Bishop's (a $20 voucher for $10) would release at midnight and the e-mails would fire off at 7:20 a.m.

At 9 p.m. Graham reviewed how we had set up the deals in the system and made a few changes. He sent an e-mail that made James and I panic for a few minutes, when he mentioned that he had reset the schedule so that the deal for Planet Fitness (a test deal we had built) would release in the morning. No! Not Planet Fitness, Bishop's! He responded quickly to the barrage of e-mails James and I sent and corrected the schedule. It was all set. I went to bed excited, as if it were Christmas Eve.

The SavingsClique.com website shortly after launch.

> **☞ TOOLS USED:**
>
> **Rolodex:** Reach out to your entire network for one last pre-launch gut check. If there are materials or a website, have them review for errors. Ask them to navigate websites, check links, call phone numbers. This is a free and vital step.
>
> **Hubspot:** Cambridge, Massachusetts-based HubSpot.com is a company that offers an amazing amount of resources to businesses that rely on the Internet. The company offers regular webinars (free) and other tools from its website. My favorite is www.websitegrader.com. In just a few seconds this website will review your website (and that of a competitor if you choose) and provide useful information on your site's search engine optimization. Before you launch a new site, running it through websitegrader.com is a must. If you have had your website built by a designer, provide the designer with the report, which will include tips on how to fix your site to them, and request changes to be made. After launch, I recommend running your site through websitegrader.com about once per month to see if there are any changes.

Afterword

The site launched, with few hiccups, on Feb. 16, 2011. The Bishop's Orchards deal sold 94 vouchers, a solid start. James and I lined up a slew of deals. I thought they would all be hits. I was wrong (again). Certain deals did really well (massage, pizza, restaurants, etc.). Some did not (retail stores).

We sped to market with our site, thank goodness. While we know that LivingSocial and Groupon will be knocking on our doorstep soon we didn't anticipate that there would soon be a gathering of local players. While none launched while I was writing this book, they are coming. Since our newspaper publishing days, James and I live by the phrase made famous by the "Godfather": "Keep your friends close and your enemies closer," and we have. We have discussed teaming up with others to create a more powerful force. We will see.

I now look at SavingsClique.com like a proud parent would look at their child after a school play. We're in the first inning of a long game, but we accomplished one of the hardest parts of becoming a business owner: the hard work of the start-up. Peering over the list of decisions that were made for this start-up is a bit daunting, but tackled one at a time (quickly), they weren't too painful.

If you have an idea, big or small, try it. Don't risk your life or family over it, but you don't want to get to a point in your life when you have that "I wish I did" moment. It might just be one of the most amazing and fulfilling parts of your life.

Please feel free to contact me if you think I can add my advice, opinions, or useless commentary to your idea. Join the entrepreneurial conversation at www.37daystolaunch.com or e-mail me at duques@wdenterprisesinc.com.